Dolphins

Kate Riggs

M000304557

Published by Creative Paperbacks
P.O. Box 227, Mankato, Minnesota 56002
Creative Paperbacks is an imprint of
The Creative Company
www.thecreativecompany.us

Design and production by Ellen Huber
Art direction by Rita Marshall
Printed in the United States of America

Photographs by Bigstock (Four Oaks, FrankU),
Dreamstime (Stephenmeese), Getty Images (Georgette
Douwma), iStockphoto (Jose Manuel Gelpi Diaz),
Shutterstock (Natalia Antonova, Willyam Bradberry,
cynoclub, Laura Lohrman Moore, Evan Shih,
ShopArtGallery), SuperStock (Minden Pictures),
Veer (defun)

Library of Congress Cataloging-in-Publication Data
Riggs, Kate.
Dolphins / by Kate Riggs.
p. cm. — (Seedlings)
Includes index.
Summary: A kindergarten-level introduction to dolphins,
covering their growth process, behaviors, the oceans they
call home, and such defining physical features as their fins.
ISBN 978-1-60818-274-9 (hardcover)
ISBN 978-0-89812-781-2 (pbk)
1. Dolphins—Juvenile literature. I. Title.

QL737.C432R55 2012
599.53—dc23   2011044739

9 8 7 6 5 4 3 2

TABLE OF CONTENTS

Hello, dolphins!

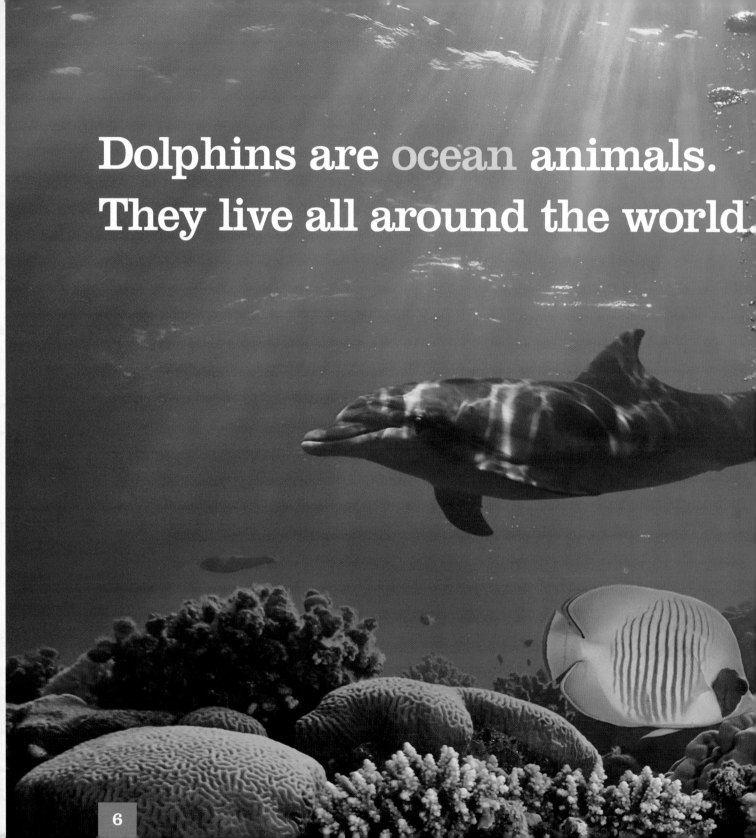

Dolphins are ocean animals.
They live all around the world.

Dolphin skin is smooth and gray.

Dolphin teeth
are small
and pointy.

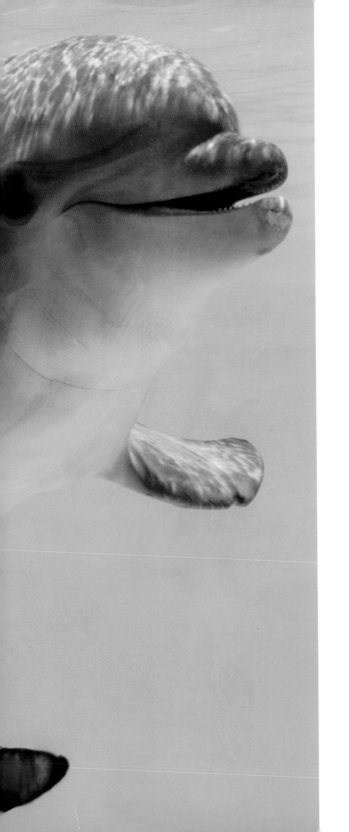

Dolphins have flippers. They breathe air through a hole on top of their head.

Dolphins eat
small fish.
They eat other
little ocean
animals, too.

A baby dolphin is called a calf. A calf lives with other dolphins in a pod.

Dolphins
like to
swim in
the ocean.
They play
and eat
all day.

Goodbye, dolphins!

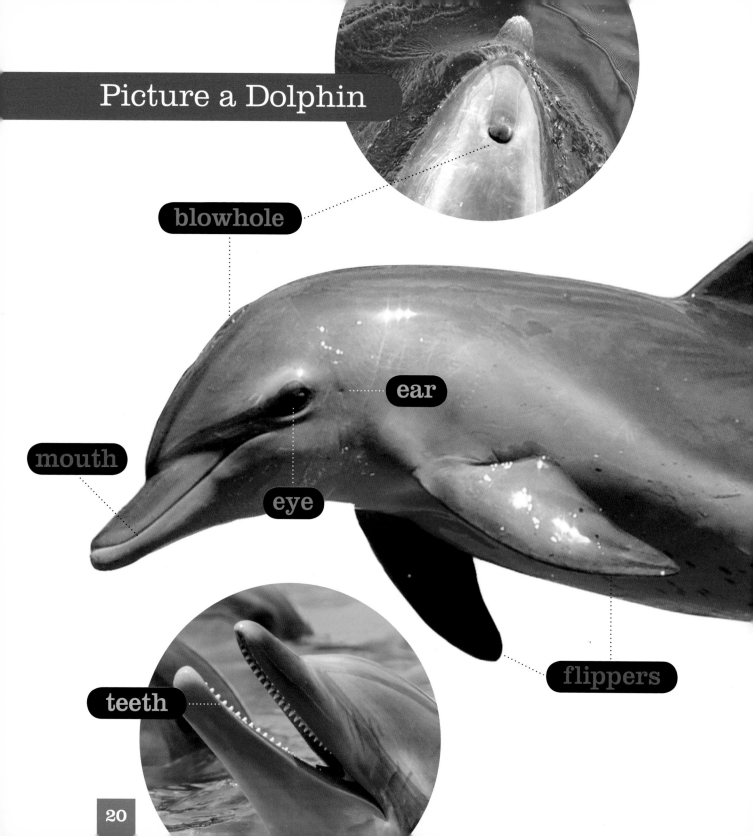

Picture a Dolphin

blowhole

ear

mouth

eye

teeth

flippers

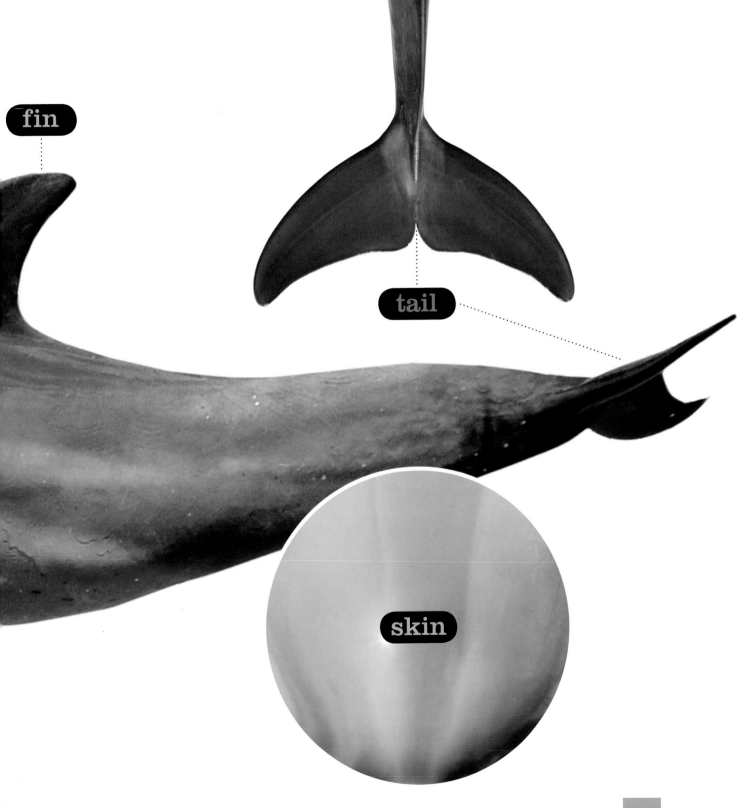

fin

tail

skin

Words to Know

flippers: flat limbs (like arms) that help dolphins swim

ocean: a big area of deep, salty water

pod: a group of dolphins that live together

Read More

Galvin, Laura Gates. *Baby Dolphin's Busy Day*.
Norwalk, Conn.: Soundprints, 2007.

Shively, Julie. *Baby Dolphin*.
Nashville: CandyCane Press, 2005.

Web Sites

Dolphin Activities and Crafts
http://www.first-school.ws/theme/animals/wild/dolphin.htm
Print out pictures to color. Then play a puzzle or do a craft!

Whale and Dolphin Coloring Book
http://www.enchantedlearning.com/crafts/books/whalebook/
Make a coloring book of your favorite whales and dolphins.

Index